I SEE YOU
DADDY

Jarvis F. Wright Sr.

To order additional copies of this book, contact:
Xlibris
844-714-8691
www.Xlibris.com
Orders@Xlibris.com

ISBN: Softcover   978-1-6641-5684-5
         EBook   978-1-6641-5683-8

Print information available on the last page

Rev. date: 02/05/2021

Luvince is visual communication firm based out of South Africa. The company offers a brand range of integrated communication solutions. In 2016, Luvince began speaking a language that expressed creativity, quality, growth and opportunity. The companies core belief is to take it to the next level every day. Luvince strives daily towards more innovative ideas and remain open to new cultures, technologies, trends and experiences. Luvince is responsible for the beautiful illustrations that you see in this book. The project was led by Nceba Majola. He can be contacted on Facebook under his name or his company's name. Those that are in South Africa can contact him with the below information:

Cel: 071 864 7330 Tel: 011 382 1332
237 Umphathi Street, Mailula Park, vosloorus,1475
Email: luvincegraphics@gmail.com

DEDICATION

This book is dedicated to my name sake, Jarvis F. Wright II.

I thought you were going to be a girl when your mom first got pregnant. Even when I found out that you were a boy, I still did not believe it. It was difficult for me to wrap my mind around the reality that God had blessed me with the extraordinary assignment of developing another man when I had just become comfortable being a man myself. It has not been long, but it has been an amazing opportunity to watch you grow. You are already making me proud.

This book is also dedicated to fathers who have embraced the serious responsibility of being a role model for their children.

You are changing the world.

DAD: MORE THAN JUST A TITLE

Substantial Denigration has come to the identity, masculinity and relevance of the man throughout history. At times and even now, these assaults appear to be unbeatable. With the rise in police violence against African American men in 2020, which is only an adjunct to the countless societal pressures that men feel, a significant question has been raised. Who will stand up for our men? We observe and acknowledge the countless strategic movements that are being initiated in response to the reproach against men; many of which are being organized and headed by women. These efforts, in my opinion, are making a significant impact. Nevertheless, my mind immediately recalls one of the most profound statements that God himself made before time began. God sees the earth that He has created and acknowledges that it is good. Yet, He also recognizes that something is missing. Man!!! Then God makes this profound statement to Himself. "Let Us make MAN in Our image." He forms the man from the dust of the earth and empowers him with the authority to act on His (God) behalf in the earth. That power and authority is still ours today.

I wonder what would happen if you and I really understood this and then conveyed this unambiguous truth to another man. Might I suggest that what is even more powerful than a woman standing up for a man is when men stand up for men. And although protests or campaigns are significant gambits to gaining an advantage over the enemies of the man, nothing tops when a father submits to the delegate assignment of being a role model for the young men that he has been called and chosen by God to raise and develop. Whether he is tasked with raising sons that live in his home or raising a son that does not live with him for whatever reason, the responsibility of raising his son must not be diminished or dismissed. You as a father must take very seriously the assignment to codirect with our God your sons in becoming men. Only this will fortify the development of our sons, ensuring that they are able to stand against the reproaches and assaults that society places on the identity, masculinity and relevance of the man.

When a boy is GUIDED into manhood, he is consequently empowered with the tools and confidence necessary to respond to the societal woes that men inevitably experience, instead of reacting to them. He is inevitably capable of standing up for himself, converting opposition into the opportunity to make an impact on society while maintaining integrity, pleasing God and representing his family well. Whereas boys often bond to their mothers right from his birth, your son's relationship with you is still the most stimulating and invigorating relationship that he will have.

In the book "Look at me Daddy," the first book of a collection of children's books I am writing called "The Affirmation Series," I mention the research on the impact that you as a father have on your children. The research steadily shows that if your children grow up under your care and guidance, they are significantly more empathetic and have greater control over the course of their lives. They also tend to do better in school and have more motivation all because of your nurturing presence. Studies reflect that there is a substantial difference in those children who lack the love or guidance of their fathers.

Now, the Father-Son relationship is unique in that it quite often does not remain the same throughout. It may experience what appears to be a roller coaster of emotions until it finally settles down at a stage that is comfortable for both. Although mentioned before, it is worth mentioning again. Baby boys depend principally on their mothers for nourishment and care, but the time spent with you is equally important. In fact, studies suggest that your interactions with your child are more stimulating, vigorous, and arousing. This is because your son looks up to you as his hero and inspiration. He altogether idolizes you and is mesmerized when his dad fixes his toy or lifts him high up in the air. You are practically viewed as stronger than Hercules and wiser than Einstein. What is most unique about the early childhood stage is that your son will try to emulate everything you do. He insists on eating like you, dressing like you, and even walking like you. He craves to spend time with you, and the smallest accolade from you is enough to make his day. In essence, it is during this stage that you gain the irreplaceable opportunity to become your child's superman. This is why it is particularly critical that you are not missing during this time.

The teenage and adulthood stages can be tough phases for both you and your son. At the teen stage, your son develops his own opinions. Clashes of opinions, arguments, and the inevitable locking of horns can occur between you and him. Your son may even appear to be losing interest in spending the same amount of time with you as during childhood. By the time your son becomes an adult, the relationship can began settling down in a comfortable zone, where both you and he respect each other's boundaries. Nevertheless, why is this not the case for many Father-Son relationships once their son reaches adulthood? Father-Son relationships are tricky. Sons idolize their fathers while they are young until he begins to realize that you are just a man, mortal and flawed. He consequently begins to assert his own identity and at times challenge his father's authority and knowledge. This is not bad; the son is learning to be independent.

However, if a father has not built a great relationship with his son prior to this stage of the relationship, he will not remain a source of influence in his son's life. Please keep this in mind when interacting with your young son. How you interact with him now will determine his willingness to maintain a relationship with you later as an adult. Sons tend not to be as forgiving as daughters concerning the adverse experiences they faced in the relationship with their father. As a father, I have a very narrow window of opportunity to preserve the longevity of the relationship with my son.

The literature suggests that the common problems impacting the relationship between a father and a son include communication, lifestyle choices, work culture, and household standards. In order to ensure our relationship with our sons is strong and intact before they become adults, we must combat these problems early on. When it comes to communication, it is important to understand that it is not enough to have abundant love for your son; you must be willing to express it. Your inability to communicate your feelings to your son can create rifts in your relationship. An example of this is seen with the father that complains that his grown-up son does not visit him often, but behind his anger is the grief of missing his child. While a son might respond to his father's anger with anger of his own, he may be more loving and understanding when he recognizes that what his father really feels is grief. We find that the general male tendency not to be emotionally vulnerable is undermining closeness. When your son has something to tell you, listen to him before giving your opinion. Also, try not to be judgmental about his choices; be understanding and supportive. When you assume the responsibility of being present to nurture your son during the early stages of the relationship, the son understands healthy masculinity. Also, there is a better chance that he will respect and strengthen the bond later in life.

In terms of the problems created through lifestyle choices, we must acknowledge that although our son is the same gender as us, they are not us. They will think differently, act differently, have different ambitions and goals and make decision that we do not agree with. This relates greatly to the issues that arise from your household standards. As the father, you may have certain beliefs and may expect your son to follow the standards of the family. Again, I tell you, it is important to understand that your son is an individual and may have his own values and beliefs, which can feel like a rejection of your customary ways of doing things. As a father, it can be hard to do so, but we must try not to take it personally. As an alternative, we can take pride in our son for having the bravery to pursue the path that feels best for him. You and your son may be complete opposites. You might like sports, while your son's idea of an outdoor activity is reading a book under the tree. Forcing him to adopt your preferences could strain the relationship and damage his self-worth. So, work to respect each other's differences to build a strong relationship.

These are just a few of the common issues that are presented in the development of a relationship with your son. There are countless others that we do not have time to address here but are worth taking the time to research at your leisure. The key to tackling these problems is to understand each other and compromise a bit. Therefore, the relationship between a father and son must be nurtured carefully at every stage of life. I cannot emphasize adequately the necessity of nurturing your son at the childhood stage especially.

I was filled with so much emotion at the birth of my daughter. How was I going to guarantee that my baby girl was always protected from the physical and emotional dangers of this world? I remember searching for gun classes in my area to sign up for. My mind was already dreading the day that I would have to meet the first boy that she would bring home to me. There was a great contrast between the birth of my daughter and the birth of my son. Not only did I feel a myriad of emotions, but there was also a co-occurrence of overwhelming anxiety. The emotion arose from the keen sense of responsibility to not only protect my son, but also develop this man child into one who would also be able to protect HIS family one day. I recognized, at the very moment of finding out that my wife was carrying my son, it was my responsibility to raise a leader.

Now please do not misunderstand me. My daughter is a leader also. A natural born leader. But when I give her away on her wedding day, it will be her responsibility to submit to the leadership of her home. I pray that the man she chooses has been developed and prepared to assume that responsibility or he will have problems. In essence, when raising a daughter, you are raising one that has the potential to lead. However, when raising a son you are raising one that has the inevitable responsibility to lead. God called men to lead. Most importantly, God called men to TEACH men how to lead. It always amazed me how women come with the innate qualities of being a woman. Yet, when a male is born, he comes almost neutral and must be trained and taught to be a man.

This explains why studies and research shows that the most important thing that a father can offer a son besides love is, HIMSELF as a role model for his son. This also explains my observation of the difference in how my daughter interacts with me versus how my son interacts with me. From the moment my daughter could talk, I heard "look at me daddy." She constantly wanted me to look at her. However, once my son began talking, he was not as interested in ensuring that I could see him. Instead, he would make sure that HE COULD SEE ME. He would just stare at me, paying close attention to me and what I was doing. As he got older, he commenced mimicking everything he saw me do. What was even more surprising was that at times he would role play the very actions and mannerisms that I used in a situation. I realized how important it was to be aware of what I was doing when I was in his presence because I was teaching him even when I was not trying to. I am my son's role model whether I like it or not. You are your son's role model whether you want to be or not.

So, as I conclude this portion of the book, here are just a few valuable lessons you as a father can teach your son. The purpose of the book is to demonstrate that these lessons are not just taught through conversation although talking to your son is great. Nevertheless, these lessons can be taught simply through your example as a role model. The children's portion of this book is designed for you to interact with your son at the childhood stage, starting a discussion about the most important lessons that you can teach him. It is filled with illustrations that demonstrate these impactful lessons and covers an array of ethnic groups. It is because fatherhood is important universally. The illustrations lead from childhood to adulthood demonstration the need to interact with our sons in every stage of their lives. Here are a few lessons that you can teach your son:

You can help your son develop the strength to face life. We all know that life will not always be a cakewalk, especially for the man today. There are challenges that boys must face when they grow up. The societal pressures to succeed at work, support the family, and to be an upstanding citizen in the community will not be easy to handle without proper guidance.

You can help your son build self-esteem and self-confidence. This can be done by involving him in some of the major decisions that affect his life. Remind him that while it is okay to fail, it is not okay to give up. Affirm his choices. Your son could face several dilemmas in life. So, teach him not to be afraid to take the least popular road. Rather than forcing him to do something you like, give your affirmation and encourage him to pursue his passion.

You can teach your son what is right. Sometimes the wrong path looks successful but can lead you to the bottom quickly. So, teach your son to choose the right path no matter how hard things get. Model for him the power of integrity and honesty. Share your personal experiences and provide reinforcement when your son makes good decisions.

You can teach your son the Importance of family. Your son will adopt many of your attitudes and behaviors about how to lead a family. Teach him the importance of spending quality time with family and valuing the family unit.

You can teach your son how to respect the women in his life. The way you treat women will lay the foundations for his future with interacting with women. Most importantly it will lay the foundation for his future romantic relationships too. Did you know that even your choice of movies and books can also communicate to your son and help him to understand your attitude towards society and women?

You can help your son understand the true definition of masculinity. Whenever he is facing a tough situation, lend a shoulder, listen patiently, and assure him it is okay to feel sad and even shed a tear or two. By doing so, you are teaching him that expressing his deep feelings will not make him less of a man. Some fathers find it difficult to express love in excessive ways, but a father's love is like the air – invisible, yet essential.

You must offer these valuable lessons to your son. However, the most important thing that you can offer your son is your presence and consistent encouragement. Can you offer friendship to your son? Can he find a friend in you? As a father, it is your responsibility to discipline your son and build their character, but your responsibility must not overshadow your love for him. While disciplining him, you must also assure your son that you can be his best friend, and he can share anything with you. After all, one day you will no longer be his manager. However, you must build a relationship with him so strong that he does not mind using you as a consultant in adulthood.

let me say very candidly that it is not hard to build a relationship with your son. One practical way to build a relationship with him is to BE THERE FOR HIM. You may be busy with work, working hard to provide for your family, but being engaged with your son is as important as financial stability for their well-being. Right from a tender age, you need to show your son that no matter what, you will always be there for him. Whether you convey it by attending their soccer games, parent-teacher meetings, or his dance recitals, just make sure you are there for him. Another way is to find common ground by discovering a common activity you both enjoy and can engage in together.

Celebrate your son's accomplishments. He may not say it, but your recognition probably means the world to him. It is every little boy's dream to make his dad proud. Every time you show appreciation to your son, he grows a bit more confident and courageous. Finally, share your experiences. As a father, you might have seen and experienced a lot. Share that wisdom with him. When you get to spend time together, use the opportunity to share your life experiences with your son. Doing this will make him feel important and happy that you trust him.

REFERENCES

Sultan, A. (2014, June 16). *WHAT MAKES SOME FATHER-SON RELATIONSHIPS SO DIFFICULT*. Retrieved from uexpress.com: https://www.uexpress.com/parents-talk-back/2014/6/16/what-makes-some-father-son-relationships-so

Vaughan, M. C. (2020, September 10). *Father-Son Relationship: Why It Matters And How It Evolves Over Time*. Retrieved from momjunction.com: https://www.momjunction.com/articles/father-son-relationship_00527515/#:~:text=The%20relationship%20between%20a%20father,his%20son%20valuable%20life%20lessons.

I see you daddy when you shave and cut your hair. It is not all about how you look my boy, but presentation shows confidence and that can get you anywhere.

I see you daddy when you are going to work every day.

"Men provide for their homes my boy. As soon as I get back home, we will go to the park to play."

I see you daddy every time you put on your tie.

"My son let me show you, then you give it a try."

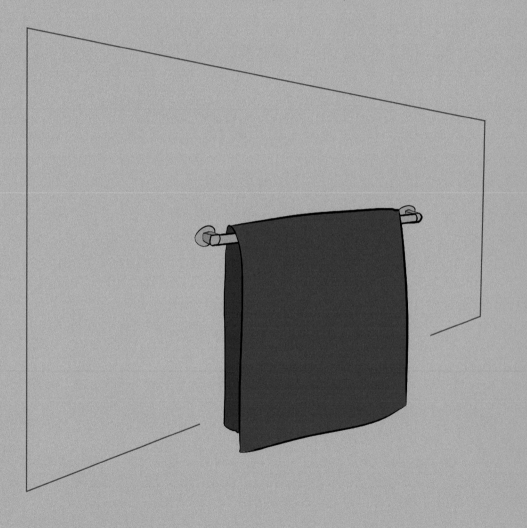

I see you daddy when you wipe
away my sister's tears.

"My boy apart of being a man is
calming your family's fears."

I saw you daddy when you apologized to that man.

"My son, only a weak person will not admit when
they are wrong. A truly strong man can."

I see you daddy when you are dancing with mommy.

"I am so glad you noticed my boy so that you, too,
will make the love of your life a priority."

I see you daddy when you are taking out the garbage and fixing the Car.

"As men, we have responsibilities and being
responsible will take you very far."

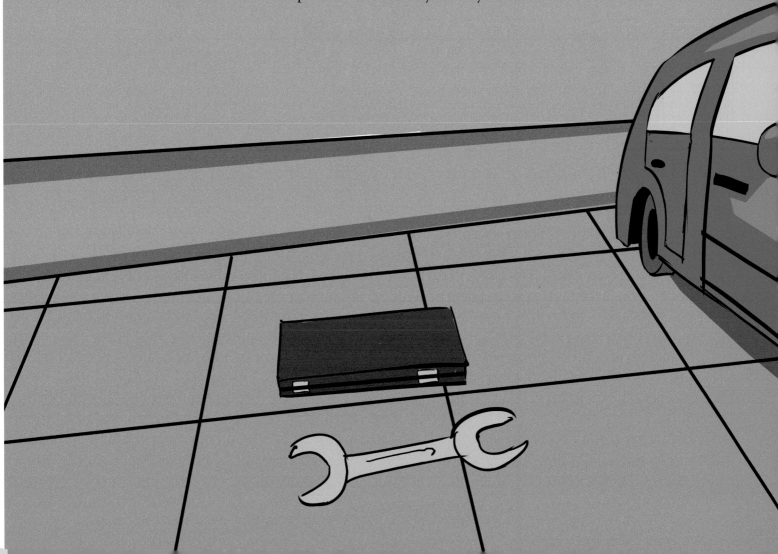

I see you daddy always helping people in need.

"You must always be able to be compassionate and generous towards others my boy. These are qualities of a man indeed."

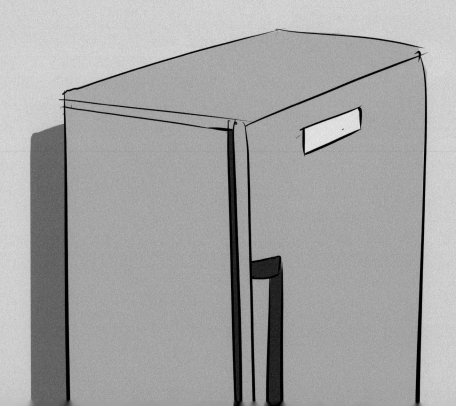

I saw you daddy, how you took care of our family and home. I am so glad I did, because now I have one of my own. You may not know it but watching you has helped me in so many ways. It helped to navigate me through life's most difficult days.

"My dear baby boy. You are smart and you are strong. You have always made me proud. I promise to be there for you just as I was when you were a child. Remember to follow the example you have seen and the lessons that you have learned. Then when life tries to knock you down, you will stand strong and firm."

Printed in the United States
By Bookmasters